Ten Poems about Cats

Candlestick Press

Published by:
Candlestick Press,
DiVersity House, 72 Nottingham Road,
Arnold, Nottingham NG5 6LF
www.candlestickpress.co.uk

Design, typesetting, print and production by DiVersity Creative Marketing Solutions Ltd., www.diversity-nottm.co.uk

First Published 2011
Reprinted 2012

ISBN 978 1 907598 08 1

Acknowledgements:
Candlestick Press wishes to thank Basil, Sybil and Mog, our three resident cats, for their contribution to this pamphlet. Double rations of fish coming your way.

The publisher thanks The Literary Trustees of Walter de la Mare and The Society of Authors as their representative for permission to print Walter de la Mare, 'Puss'; Anna Wigley and Gomer Press for 'The Missing Cats of Roath' from *Waking in Winter*, Gomer Press, 2009; Anne Stevenson and Bloodaxe Books for 'Clydie is dead!' from *Poems 1955-2005*, Bloodaxe Books, 2005; Jen Hadfield and Bloodaxe Books for 'In the same way' from *Nigh-No-Place*, Bloodaxe Books, 2008. Thom Gunn, 'Apartment Cats', is from *Collected Poems*, Faber and Faber Ltd, 1993, Elizabeth Coatsworth, 'On a Night of Snow' is printed by permission of The Marsh Agency Ltd on behalf of the Estate of Elizabeth Coatsworth and 'Tabby' is printed by permission of Curtis Brown and Grace Nichols, © Grace Nichols, 2000.

Where poets are no longer living, their dates are given.

Candlestick Press is making a donation from profits to Cats Protection, the UK's leading cat welfare charity which helps 215,000 cats and kittens each year through a national network of 256 volunteer-run branches and 30 Adoption Centres.

For more information, visit www.cats.org.uk

Contents **Page**

Introduction

We three Candlestick Cats were delighted to be asked to write the Introduction to *Ten Poems about Cats*. Cats have provided writers and artists with inspiration since Ancient Egypt, when we weren't just adored – we were considered holy. Aesop featured us in a couple of his Fables and in thirteenth-century England, we were the only animals that were allowed as pets for nuns. Monks kept us too - you can find pictures of us in medieval illuminated manuscripts. In brief, we have the kind of literary and artistic ancestry other pets (think gerbil) would die for.

The poems we helped our owners to select for inclusion in this pamphlet range across centuries, seasons and styles. We wanted to show the diversity of cat poetry and hence made some unusual choices to expand the knowledge and understanding of cats. Some readers may be surprised at the absence of any poems from T S Eliot's *Old Possum's Book of Practical Cats*. There's a simple explanation for this; we abhor practicality. We ourselves are never knowingly practical. Also, those particular practical cats get everywhere and don't require any introduction from us. Instead, we've chosen some less well-known poems; for example, poems by Anna Wigley and Jen Hadfield, and one by Thom Gunn about his kittens. We probably wouldn't have put up with the antics of his kittens, but he seemed to find them entertaining enough. We even steeled ourselves to include Anne Stevenson's beautiful poem about a cat that has died. In short, we hope that you find as many different takes on cats as can be fitted into ten poems.

We're pleased that our owners are going to make a donation from their profits to Cats Protection, not least since one of us (Mog) was a rescue cat and glad to be given a new home where food is plentiful and beds are soft. Talking of which…

Basil, Sybil and Mog, The Candlestick Cats

The Cat of Cats

I am the cat of cats. I am
The everlasting cat!
Cunning, and old, and sleek as jam,
The everlasting cat!
I hunt vermin in the night –
The everlasting cat!
For I see best without the light –
The everlasting cat!

William Brighty Rands (1823 – 1882)

On a Night of Snow

Cat, if you go outdoors, you must walk in the snow.
You will come back with little white shoes on your feet,
little white shoes of snow that have heels of sleet.
Stay by the fire, my Cat. Lie still, do not go.
See how the flames are leaping and hissing low,
I will bring you a saucer of milk like a marguerite,
so white and so smooth, so spherical and so sweet –
stay with me, Cat. Outdoors the wild winds blow.

Outdoors the wild winds blow, Mistress, and dark is the night,
strange voices cry in the trees, intoning strange lore,
and more than cats move, lit by our eyes' green light,
on silent feet where the meadow grasses hang hoar –
Mistress, there are portents abroad of magic and might,
and things that are yet to be done. Open the door!

Elizabeth Coatsworth (1893 – 1986)

Apartment Cats

The Girls wake, stretch, and pad up to the door.
They rub my leg and purr:
One sniffs around my shoe,
Rich with an outside smell,
The other rolls back on the floor –
White bib exposed, and stomach of soft fur.

Now, more awake, they re-enact Ben Hur
Along the corridor,
Wheel, gallop; as they do,
Their noses twitching still,
Their eyes get wild, their bodies tense,
Their usual prudence seemingly withdraws.

And then they wrestle: parry, lock of paws,
Blind hug of close defence,
Tail-thump, and smothered mew.
If either, though, feels claws,
She abruptly rises, knowing well
How to stalk off in wise indifference.

Thom Gunn (1929 – 2004)

The Retired Cat

A poet's cat, sedate and grave
As poet well could wish to have,
Was much addicted to inquire
For nooks to which she might retire,
And where, secure as mouse in chink,
She might repose, or sit and think.
A drawer, it chanced, at the bottom lined,
With linen of the softest kind,
With such as merchants introduce
From India, for the ladies' use;
A drawer, impending o'er the rest,
Half open in the topmost chest,
Of depth enough and none to spare,
Invited her to slumber there;
Puss with delight beyond expression,
Surveyed the scene and took possession.

William Cowper (1731 – 1800)

Tabby

My cat is all concentrated tiger.
I can only imagine the thousands
of millions of years
it must have taken to perfect her.
Growing smaller and smaller
with each evolution.
Growing more and more refined
and even-tempered under her fur.

See how she constantly licks
and grooms herself all over?

A small Queen of Sheba
stamping everywhere her padded
signature – a royal reminder
of the days she was a full-blown tiger.
Older O much older than Egypt.

Now, just look at her –
my grey and black tabby, stepping lightly,
emerging head first from between
the green garden stalks –

Ancient and new as the birth of a star.

Grace Nichols

The Missing Cats of Roath

Tacked to the makeshift noticeboards
of lamp-posts and trees,
their blurred, faded faces peer out
at passing strangers, like whiskered babies
stolen from their prams;
or once-prosperous refugees,
now wandering the world of back lanes
barefoot, without a passport or a name.
They are the missing cats of Roath,
the lost links in a chain of cats
that curls from Angus to Arabella Street
and back; cats guarding their dignity
in smutty gutters, on crumbling walls,
or framed in windows where once a day
a lozenge of sunlight falls.
Please check your garages and sheds
the posters plead, for Tigger, Molly and Fred,
for Nipper, Fluffy and Nutmeg,
who may be kipping there under an old rake
in a nest of cobwebs, smeared with oil,
already getting that mangy look, those haunted eyes,
reverting to feral versions of themselves,
slaking their thirst on rain puddles,
and after years of indolence and Kit-e-Kat,
pricking their ears at tiny scurryings
and learning, at last, to hunt.
But somehow they never turn up,
the missing cats of Roath.
They are too numerous; it can't be chance
that so many end like this: famous for a week,
their pictures hung up as talismans, idols,
messages to the gods.
Somewhere they congregate, and smile at us.
Somewhere they curl into perfect circles, and wait.

Anna Wigley

Clydie is dead!

Our lar, our little mammal.
Though his last day didn't believe it.
It kept on moving at its usual heartless pace
over and around a hollow cat-space.

We buried him by the toolshed.
The cat flap wouldn't believe it,
so we sealed its chattering mouth.
We seized and scrubbed his feeding bowls
and sent them to a far shelf.

The fact is, nothing in the house could bear it
when Clyde dropped out of himself…
who waxed loquacious on the subject of roast meat
and cats' rights, who took favours
from my fingers at mealtimes as just deserts,
who always kept his dress-shirt spinnaker-white
while extending an urgent tongue to his tabby parts;
who reserved for himself, every morning,
a place on a lap, whereon for a while he might
subdue a human; upon whose face
the cat-painter's brush had slipped a little
applying the Chinese white; for which he received
in compensation, huge Indonesian eyes –
polished jet in a setting of crinkled topaz;

whose tail was so long he could wrap himself up in it;
who could fill with his length, without exertion,
the entire shelf over the radiator;
who was adept at the art of excretion,
and discreet as to the burying of personal treasure.

Dear, wise Clyde, who after tyrannical Bonnie died,
thrived in her absence, Hadrian after Domitian,
you will never again rule us by vocative law,
or pull back the bedclothes at six with a firm paw,
or bemoan the indignities of travelling by car,
or flourish an upright tail on crepuscular walks,
no, nor compile statistics on the field mice of Wales.

Pwllymarch was your chief estate,
you whom Oxford made and Cambridge unmade,
though Hay-on-Wye and Durham made you great.
Much travelled, valuable, voluble Clyde,
who said so much, yet never spoke a word,
requiescat.

Anne Stevenson

In the same way

In the same way she cries at the kitchen door
and I slip her and she runs into circular squalls of rain

and she cries at the kitchen door
with snailtracks of rain in her muscular fur
so I open up and she runs in singing

and she cries at the kitchen door
so I open up and she crouches
then sprints into the wind

and the wind cries at the kitchen door
so I open up and call and call

and she doesn't run in but the wind does,
with rain, a squall of claws –

in the same dogged, idiotic way
I open up, send Goodnight across the brae,

and the wind canters in
and she with a wild carol

and all the night hail
melted gleaming in her furs

Jen Hadfield

Two Nursery Rhymes

I Love Little Pussy

I love little Pussy, her coat is so warm;
And if I don't hurt her she'll do me no harm.
So I'll not pull her tail, nor drive her away,
But Pussy and I very gently will play.

She shall sit by my side, and I'll give her some food;
And she'll love me because I am gentle and good.
I'll pat little Pussy and then she will purr,
And thus show her thanks for my kindness to her.

I'll not pinch her ears, nor tread on her paw,
Lest I should provoke her to use her sharp claw;
I never will vex her, nor make her displeased,
For Pussy can't bear to be worried or teased.

Anon

Pussy Cat, Pussy Cat

Pussy Cat, Pussy Cat, where have you been?
I've been to London to visit the Queen.
Pussy Cat, Pussy Cat, what did you there?
I frightened a little mouse under the chair.

Anon

Puss

Puss loves man's winter fire
Now that the sun so soon
Leaves the hours cold it warmed
In burning June.

She purrs full length before
The heaped-up hissing blaze,
Drowsy in slumber down
Her head she lays.

While he with whom she dwells
Sits snug in his inglenook,
Stretches his legs to the flame
And reads his book.

Walter de la Mare (1873 – 1956)